SERENADE

OF

THOUGHTS

By

Jeardine Q. Santos, Ed.D

COPYRIGHT © 2022 SERENADE OF THOUGHTS
By Jeardine Q. Santos

Edited by Marie Ezekiel
Designed by Tess Ritumalta

ISBN:
Softbound/Paperback-978-621-470-262-6
Hardbound-978-621-470-263-3
MOBI/KINDLE-978-621-470-264-0

Published by:
Poetry Planet Book Publishing House
Rosario, Pozorrubio, Pangasinan, Philippines
Contact No.: 09554960044
Email: maritesritumalta@gmail.com

DEDICATION

The author wholeheartedly dedicates this book to
those who have provided the inspiration
and encouragement ;
To her loving parents , Mrs Adelaida O. Quenano and
late Federico P. Quenano;
Her beloved husband Gemwell R. Santos
for his practical and cheerful disposition;
Jenea Ghem, Tristan Lhee, Ken Amhir and Jhulio
Jemkhenlee,
her kids, her driving force and inspiration;
To her brothers,
Frederick, Vincent, and Ferdinand
and her sisters
Fedelaine, Han Suyen, Saranay, Zarina and Fedmina,
for their love support and motivation.
To her mentor/adviser
Isidra R. Cagatan
for her constant encouragement and valuable
insights.

ACKNOWLEDGEMENT

The author is expressing her warm gratitude to the following persons;

Mrs. Isidra A. Cagatan, for her constant encouragement, brilliant suggestions, and valuable insights to improve this book;

Jenea Ghem, her daughter, for her unselfish support, valuable suggestions, and sharing her knowledge and technical expertise;

Tristan Lhee, Ken Amhir, and Jhulio Jemkhenlee her sons for the continuous support and understanding.

Gemwell Santos, her supportive and loving husband, for his untiring support, and deep affectionate concern in the completion of this book.

Her mother Adelaida O. Quenano for her love and invaluable supervision;

Her sisters and brothers for their unfailing spiritual and moral support during the entire process;

Finally, the **Almighty Father** whose countless blessings have turned a formidable task into reality.

TABLE OF CONTENTS

A PROMISE OF GENUINE LOVE

Yesterday, today, and tomorrow here we are
Loving tenderly as we get closer our hearts
You are my loving buddy and so do I am my
sweetheart
In all aspects of life together we stand for our part.

I love you as you love me too
I am very proud to show
To the world of what I feel for you
My man, my dear one we are a duo.

A loving husband and the father of my two
The genuine love that we share now and so
Not ephemeral but lasting forever true
The best tremendous feeling of love I can do.

A promise of genuine love until we get the oldest
Holding one another as we walk on the beach
Renewing our love yearly as we wish
Sharing the loving feeling now and always.

We get the power of love
From God our Father above
We fly freely like a sweet dove
My darling, my dear one the only one I have.

MERRY CHRISTMAS

Christ the King was born
On Bethlehem in the very early morn
His mother was wandering to find a place to give him
birth
No one liked them to accept with mirth.

From very far there he was on cattle place
Laying beneath the lambs and some horses
This was showing a very humble case
That our saviour was born in a situation of the poorest.

The angels all are rejoicing
They were all singing
With a hymn so loud and solemn
All the bells are ringing.

Halleluiah let's all be happy
Jesus our Saviour is here today
Let's celebrate and by repenting our sins daily
Christmas is here let's be merry.

NEW NORMAL

The world experiences a new life trend
This is because of the dangerous Covid nineteen
It seems to halt us for a while frightened
With lockdowns and series of quarantines.

Many of us lost jobs and some with their loved ones
The virus is so terrific and horrible one
That keeps us staying at home
To be safe away from anyone.

Everyone wears a face mask and face shield
We keep our smiles within for a while
No to togetherness of individuals and yield
We can see all while an empty field.

Our school definitely has no children
They are studying at home with their parents
Using different modalities to learn
Online, modular, or blended learning.

This is unusual for all of us in this world
But we have to adapt this in action, not by word
To survive and surpass this New Normal to uphold
We tend to be flexible in this we unfold.

New Normal ways of life we have to adjust
In this we have to abide, we must.
Only God can save and tell us
When to end this situation let's pray it will end at last.

YOU ARE THE ONE

You lead us into the brightness of life
You surpassed all the life's strife
Your struggles were paid off you fight
Against all odds you were alone but you did it right.

You are the one leading us to a better future
You must be our inspiration our leader in nature
Your words and actions were once belittled but you
captured
Their hearts and understanding in favor of yours.

Cause you are the epitome of a courageous heart
You try to conquer the world with your human touch
Your struggles were transformed into triumphant
Now you succeed over the hindrance cause you are
the one

No matter how difficult is the situation
Still, you go on and looking for the solution
Now here you are on the pedestal we all look you on
Your success is just an event but you are unique on
your own.

You are the one that elevates our humanity
We adore you so much despite the disparity
Uniting the different races beyond universality
Towards the common goals with transparency.

POETRY IS THE SISTER OF SORROW

In my loneliness, you are my peeping light of hope
That gives me fully a very sustaining spark of proof
I really cannot prevent and naturally cope
This awesome feeling of sorrowful manifestation of
being aloft.

Because of my poetry I standstill tall and smiling
To the life's journey that keeps on hindering
No matter how strong I am it keeps me affecting
To the avenue of a true and real experiencing

OH! Poetry though you are a sister of sorrow
Yes let me stay now and tomorrow
But you are the delight of a hopeless sparrow
Who lends a light of a bright morning through.

HELLO DECEMBER

Christmas is here at our door
The coming of our dearest Savior
Let us rejoice and bring love into our home
A very Merry Christmas is just around.

December is the most awaited month of the year
Hello! we are so excited to meet you dear
What amazing are the presents you give us here
How enjoying is every day we think of it there.

A very Merry Christmas everyone is longing
Happiness and joy it brings
A special celebration that we can beyond comparing
An extraordinary love that touches our inner being.

Every individual is to keep on preparing
For the Lord Jesus coming
The essence of why we are celebrating
Not for whatever earthly matters it keeps us exciting.

The bells around are ringing
Sweet music for caroling
That invites our vivacious feelings
The bongacious decors on the walls and buildings.

Christmas is here in the Philippines
In every corner of the world its inherent
But for us, it's far different
For we give all and love is evident.

December is the last month of the year
Here we are having a party here and there
But whatever we do we must remember
The very reason why we celebrate Christmas here.

Rich or poor have a celebration
On the street or in a condominium
In the city or the places of the interior
Wherever they may be in the world.

THE BUTTERFLIES

In a garden of flowers
I can see some fliers
They are the wondrous butterflies
Flying in the garden of lovers.

Different colors that resemble
They are so lovely and adorable
They are alluring and meaningful
That captivates our attention so double.

Fly, fly like a butterfly
In the midst of a captivating sky
Fly up to the highest height
That no one can reach but the light.

A submissive wind blows in the east
A coordinating colors that match
The yelling sound that alleviates
The adorable beauty that invites.

Yeah you are really wondrous
In the sense of growing glows
In your existence that arose
The maturity that grows.

The metamorphosis of a butterfly
Is something that tells us why
From a larva to a caterpillar then to a lovable butterfly
So lovely that surrounds us day and night.

Flying and landing on a lovely flower
They keep on transferring from one another
The flying colors of a magical flier
That gives the essence of their existence in the air.

I love to watch you over there
I am the envy of your freedom anywhere
You are lively but free from hunger
You only sip the sweetness of a lovely flower.

By and by you can catch the rising sun
You are fully equipped with love upon
That somehow be duplicated by some
Who are longing for a habitat for everyone.

TAKE ME NOW

On a huge crowd of a promised land
Here I am thinking about you Hernan
Waiting for your love from Dapitan
Yes Oh, I found my truest love as I look upon.

Take me now I'm free to fly with you
In every space, I'm ready to go
That's how we really do
Because I truly love you.

I am mot a romantic gal
But with you, I make it my guy
We become one and multiplied
The two boys are the evidence.

I love you as you take me now
You love me too and we took a vow
We hand in hand go along the row
The straight path of loving with no boundary of an
arrow.

I commit and dedicate myself to you
Our love grew old as we do
But the capacity of loving never go
We are still the same as we were as I said I do.

The blessing of God to us continue
As we follow the life having me and you
You are my life and I is yours
I love you forever my love as if we are new.

MY FATHER DEAREST HAPPY BIRTHDAY!

My beloved father was my first teacher
He taught me how to write some letters
He led me to say a prayer
He was a very good father ever.

In my childhood, I was very happy
With my father as my tutor every day
The enthusiastic coach who gave lessons of life daily
Valuable advices that let me grow respectfully.

He was a guide to pass life's challenges
He always supported me to take chances
He was my best friend that never changes
He was my shield when troubles or crossroads
appears.

My beloved Papa my confidante
He listened to my stories sadly or merrily
He was my protector and cheerer all the way
He was an action man who is ready to help the
community.

He was my storyteller the best father on Earth
No matter what might they say, I love my father
When I'm down I just call him out there
And he immediately sends an answer.

Papa 18 years ago that you were with us
Some people say that you were so radical
But for me, you were a man of trust
Of great principled human that can't be put to dust

I inherit your values a lot.
For those long years that you went away
Your teachings remain in my heart wilfully
Your good deeds were engraved deeply

Your footprints were followed carefully.
That's how meaningful you were
How essential you were forever
We love you, we miss you beloved father

Please protect us though you are in nowhere.
Pray that Mama will live longer
So that we can give the best to her
Your sweet darling our loving mother
We want to be with her for longer years.

A SHADY AFTERNOON

On the street, you can feel a canopy
That covers your tone of skinny
Sheltered with passionate recovery
That touches the pure heart of alienated amenity.

The shady afternoon at riverside
Wow! makes my eyes so wide
Astonished with changes all while
The impossible was so possible in the Commonwealth
life.

The dazzling air touches my skin
I felt assured to walk within
My darling protects me every now and then
We are surely cared for by our Father in heaven.

So sweet to listen to the homily
Of the Holy mass today
Husband and wife should live in harmony
That's what reminds us to stay strong and happy.

Everything connects on a shady afternoon
The happiness that keeps us on
The married life of us with God upon
Yes, we merrily live and abide by your command.

LAUGHTER

When you laugh, happiness is overloaded
When you frown, sadness is uploaded
That can make you degraded
For the unethical act is added.

Laugh oh laugh my friend
Show kindness and make it happen
For all the burdens to be lessened
Uplift your soul and kept strengthened.

In every corner of the world
Shout out with an empathic word
Laugh oh laugh aloud
The way that makes you proud.

Diminish the negativism
Increase the positivism
Always uphold patriotism
Filipino is gaily with a mannerism.

Intact your goal at hand
Do it nicely for a fun
Love and share as you can
Di not look back sadly at damn.

BE DECISIVE

Now is the time to make an important decision
Go or not in the field of the rainy season
The children the miniature on the street will go on
In the flood, they'll swim on

Why don't you observe the situation?
The heavy rains go on and on
It's good for you lying in a room of aircon
While these children seek education.

Are on the floody street keeping on
They are wet with all parents' protection
Not enough because rain soothes on
Why don't you give your decision?

Many times you keep us on frustration
The children and everybody had gone on
Facing the dangerous situation
Only in the late afternoon that you gave your decision.

We are all the servants of God
We don't want to miss our duty to God
We don't aim to rest on the day of work
For our clients who are still small.

So we are pleading to give your decision on time
So that these mini creatures won't get wet on the line
We want them to be fine
Please decide to save lives and be kind.

GOOD MORNING LORD

Thank you for your numerous glorious blessings
Sorry for all the wrongdoings
We supposed to do the good things
And discard the non-sense

Lord, we appeal to you Father Almighty
To pursue your patience in a mystical way
We embrace all the consequences of our mistakes
humbly
We have no right to complain but accept the reality.

Do not permit us to lose in the high way of life
Keep us tightly in your dominion for us to survive
Cleanse the path that we walk along to revive
Give us assurance of strong faith as we live.

We fear nothing for we know you are here
We don't have to worry about anything for you are our
provider
Our lives become secured and simpler
Which you blessed us anywhere.

Take away the heavy loads that some of us disturb
Awaken us with songs of hope
Call us with your loud assuring voice
Cover us with your canopy so that nothing can annoy
us.

Lord at all times keep us a whole
With no double thoughts at all
Let us focus on only one Lord God
And remind us that Earthly matters don't last.

A MIDNIGHT PRAYER

Lord, thank you for bringing us in the midnight
The silence and the tranquillity of light
The sweet sound of sleep so tight
The promising tomorrow that lies beside.

Let the coming day awaits us successfully
That it may touch us spiritually
Holding us with favor and love morally
So we could go on our mission tactfully.

Our past may give us a gauge of righteousness
That reminds us of being sons and daughters
Enlighten us to the words of wisdom and
completeness
That taps us every time we do some mistakes.

Let the diminutive creatures around us propagate
With a correct and proper way to disseminate
May they live in accordance with your will and inherit
The true essence of living here on Earth.

We may uphold your ten commandments
Abiding it fully with respect and no discernment
We may be accretive to comply with all the Holy
sacraments
That strengthens our being solid Christians. Amen

SUMMER BREEZE

I smell the aroma of the summer breeze
I can sense the fragrance of the lovely roses
How sweet that captivates my sweet caress
So annoying that I almost forget myself.

Summer breeze, so amplifying in my ears
So hot that I release all my perspire
So reminiscing that I treasure all my memoirs
So inviting that I can't say no but yes all over.

One summer breeze that blew me out
I was still young and had a big mouth
I had to scatter all my baggy doubts
But I had to listen to the murmuring voice aloud.

Oh! so awesome a numerous flattering clouds
Are aligned row by row across the sunny mount
So refreshing to think of them all around
But somehow I can't afford to reach them out.

On the other side of the universe
Here comes the northern hemisphere
Looking it up is so nice and clear
The magnificent shadow dancing up there.

In the twilight of summer days up high
I can't resist myself I can't deny
Nothing falls in my mind but just sigh
This is the ultimate exit of a happy night.

SICKNESS PLEASE KEEP AWAY FROM ME

I can feel my weakened muscles
The aching left shoulder has almost no force
The pain that penetrates to the bones
I try to calm myself, Cindy! Go don't stumble.

We are about to go to church
Getting ready to praise you, Lord
I keep on conditioning myself that I'm alright
Though I feel something uncertain

My palms are warm and the aching shoulder goes
These are usual feelings as I go through a
menopausal stage
But this time my back head coordinates
Daddy, I said I have to take a rest.

Yesterday all day long I rested
I canceled all my activities
There are a lot of things I did before that I missed
I'm becoming weaker since I stepped into my fifties.

I just pray to God these are all temporary
I don't want to be a baggage to my family
My sons are still young to carry me
Cheer up Cindy these are just a test and be healthy.

As I laid down in bed I got my phone
I still want to share my story on
My husband stops me from holding my phone
But my playful fingers still write a poem.

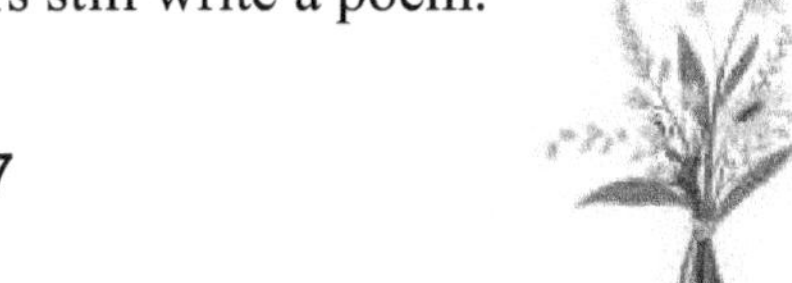

Faith in God gives me more hope
If you can read this friend please take a look
Have a prayer for all of us and be strong
Sickness is only a mindset condition.

EDUCATOR'S LIFE

I am a teacher
I live like a preacher
My heart beats for my pupils
This makes me happy so well.

As an educator, I swear
That throughout my life I serve
To my dearest learners
Who needs my care so tender.

My life is dedicated to my profession I took the oath
Forever I will share my expertise to spread out
The true essence of learning to my pupils' suit
This won't change till I get too old.

As an individual, challenges are just around
There are a lot of trials on the ground
But I have a strong determination
To pursue my vision and mission.

I have to live a balanced life
My family and career in line
Yes it's too difficult to abide
But more or less I get it right.

Educator's life is not easy
I should be firmed in what I say
I must be a model to their innocent memory
Who are watching my steps every day.

What I show to them are their guide
My words and action should be fine
In my mistake, they might mislead
For they think I'm always correct.

I can make or unmake their future
Every praise I do to them captures
The tangible mindset that nurtures
Their trusts and beliefs in me occur.

This job of mine needs more sacrifices
This won't make me rich while in practice
But the payback is so worthwhile
Heavenly happiness that gives me a wide smile.

MIDNIGHT DEW

Wintertime in a tropical place
Like our country the Philippines
Somehow I dream to feel like this
Midnight dew blows me, please.

In the polar places, they have snow
They are more or less feeling so cold
Their feathery jackets keep them warm but low
The rock of ice surrounds them so.

Midnight dew what can I do?
To make you feel that I am true
How can I convince you?
I am just a mediocre in this midtown glow.

In every cooling nook, you stay
I am conveying a message you say
But the cold penetrates my whole body
Trying to stop my breath but I disagree.

The moist and hydrogenic power of you
Soothes my nerves and taps me too
So cold, so demanding to capture my whole life
through
So amazing that keeps me live all it though.

The weather and climate encompass
The stars and other terrestrials
All of them celebrate the midnight dew that passes
For it gives them a chilling effect that lasts.

You are just temporary as I know
But the memoirs you give are somehow longing too
The scents of midnight dew
Is something everlasting that takes a vow.

A DAY OF HEARTS

The heart is a pumping station of the body
It allows the blood to flow all the way
The blood goes in and out from it oh yeah!
February 14 is a celebration of the hearts' day.

What's in the heart that makes us feel loved
It's a mysterious way that we have
A scientific fact differs from God
The function of the heart is a magnetic act.

We are of different races and we vary in culture and
tradition
But the feeling we have is a standard rule
Heart to heart talk we must do it sincerely at all
Heart, you are a body part that has nothing to compare
as a whole.

Get into the apple shape below the throat
Above the stomach, the heart lies about
Two hearts that beat as one
Have you heard this parable?

No, it's not a parable but true to all.
Sharing one's love story
Is an honest deed we feel today
Be careful with a love that bears actually

For they have no wings but fly away.
A day of hearts please come with me
To the one we love we must be proud each day
A love that lasts, a gift from God Almighty

STEADFAST

We are the sons and daughters of God
We belong to him whatever on Earth we tagged
What level we may have
My brothers and sisters steadfast

In this fragile world, we may not last
But to Father God, we are all equal
We may be the least brethren in their eyes
But to God, we are so special

We can not measure our faith on how often we kneel
and cry in front of the altar
And how many masses we attend every day to show
who we are
Nor how much we give to the offertory to show our
sympathy to others
But in ourselves, we know very much who we are.

Truly, steadfast to God only
By doing good so sincerely
Every day is a gift of God dearly
believe in Him not by showing in a halfway

MERRY CHRISTMAS

This is a season to give love
To share with others what you have
To celebrate the birth of our savior
Who is sent to us by Father God.

This is not only for one day
This is for every day as we live a day
The message of love to the needy
Who really longs for our care and subsidy.

Give love to the least individual
Do not count your help but extend as usual
The sincerest intention as you do the mission of
virtual
Be content with what God has showered you in
actuality.

How happy we are if we could do good
No matter how big or less to the neighborhood
As long as it comes from the heart of brotherhood
The meaning of Christmas is the ultimate answer to
the queries along the road.

Don't stop there, pursue your mission
For you have made a lonely heart to shine
To boost self-esteem and to live life moving
The last thing you did in them counts

Be a living and truest inspiration.
Merry Christmas have a special touch
To someone, to everyone, to the one who needed it
much
Even a single shoulder patch can do a lot

It can give a deeper meaning to survive at that.
Christmas is not a gift of your choice
Is not only a material thing that makes you rejoice
It's something that echoes a golden voice

Of love and manifested the most essential noise.
Jesus is the reason for this season
Let us follow his footsteps as shown
Loving one another and humbling yourself alone
Can be an example that God wants us to go on.

IF I HAVE TO WRITE A POEM

I have to write it for God my creator
For my family who is always my protector
For my friends who are my sincere collaborators
For my colleagues who are my co-innovators

I write a poem to express my being me
I write to live a life full of fantasy
I love to share a masterpiece I made a day to day
This is the least thing I know I can be.

If I have to write anything in this world
I have to use my own words
The one that defines my life so far and loud
That waves you away while I am on top of the cloud.

THE DANCING DAFFODILS

I take a walk in the early morn
In a place where I was born
I can see nobody but am alone
Except for the fresh air that blows around

In nearby meadows that surround me
It is a habitat of birds that crowds as I can see
A beautiful flower strikes my sight and invites me
Dancing in the blown air with a busy bee.

Oh how I love to keep my eyes on thee
It's amazing to be in this kind of place and stay
To meditate and go dancing them silently
Peace of mind and be what you want to be.

The dancing daffodils keep inviting me
The lovely shape of their flowers invades my privacy
I stop walking and talk to them invasively
I said to them you know to you I am envy.

For your ultimate happiness so genuine
No one can take it away from you I swear in
Keep dancing with the blow of the wind
And the nature that adapts you swaying.

Dancing daffodils bye for now
I pursue my journey but my feet say no oh how?
I can't take away from your sweet and lovely bow
But no matter what I should go but remember my
vow.

At a right time, I must return
To disclose your hidden beau to the world
So that everyone can take a chance on board
Exerting efforts and taking a parting word.

VIVACIOUS FEELINGS!

Expressing happiness in the way you are
The proudness of something you get from
The feeling of contentment because you care for
someone
The honest behavior you bestow in the crowd.

Viva! The bell rings in joyous moments
Christmas time is fast approaching
The Savior lay on the Belen of Bethlehem
Come on let's prepare for his coming.

The precursor came before Him
Let's rejoice and get ready all the time
Jesus our savior our king is about to be sent
Our hearts and deeds would be cleansed.

Our vivacious feelings bring us forth
The all-out and meaningful support
To the Son of God our Savior
Who saved us from the sins of ours.

This is the time to forgive
To forget the one whom you have offended
Putting love in our inner being
Live vivaciously with God as your guide in your
living.

UNNOTICED THOUGHTS

Come on thinking of nothing
Sending and replicating but so obligating
Simplifying the ideas, so complicating
Walk on the pavement of a crazy thing.

OH! No, you have just unnoticed thoughts
Think aloud and bring the lost in truths
We might exist in the lonely crowd
Nobody looks back in yours.

How sad you won't be remembered by some in the
new rules
In the middle of your days becoming old
Bring forth the moments you are told
Listen to the whisper of the cloud.

You can guess how does it looks like
When you are gone in the wilderness
Staying aware of some techniques
But you are gulped out of selfishness.

Unnoticed thoughts went by
No need for you to hide
Go out and expose your side
Begin to smile with a sigh.

Being not heard when you shout out
Having a harsh voice about
Losing yourself and not so tout
Take it and be thankful for the unnoticed thought.

STANDSTILL

Beneath the stormy day
Standstill God will hold you firmly
Never attempt to go away
Instead, have a grip on him so closely.
Standstill whatever ambiguities

You will never be directed to zigzag ways
No matter what, God is your guide in the high ways
Be faithful, have self-confidence and you'll never lose
your ways.
Standstill, be full of positive vibes

Even in the moment of shameful thoughts that you
almost cried
Standstill never show your weaknesses that lied
Have full delectation be in your deeds abide.
Standstill in the midst of the crowd that crowns the
clouds

Invite the blessings of the Almighty God
Stay harmless and live the commandments of God
For you will be forever granted security that lasts.

Standstill listen to your heartbeats
What do they say to your ears?
Go on towards the straight path
And God be with you for a million ways that count.

MY BELOVED PAPA'S BIRTHDAY

I always reminisce the moment
When you were still with us on Earth
The love you bestowed on us was nothing to compare
I love you dearest Papa Rest in peace there.

You were a stage father
Presented in all school affairs
Attending the meetings here and there
You were always proud of me and my sister.

You did everything for the family
You made the night a day
You did not rest to chase an opportunity
For us, you did not stop even a holiday.

My love and respect to you dear father
Continues to flow until the end of my life here
You taught me how to be strong and firm
To live life simply as a fighter.

Against poverty and non-sense
So did follow your footprints
Your dedication and hard work were beyond forever
Til your borrowed life ends and awake never.

Your legacy in our family
And to the barangay, you served fully
You marked a man of legendary
That gives us a norm of being straight and not a bully.

YESTERDAY WHEN I WAS YOUNG

I never stop thinking about how I could help my
parents
Now that I'm old enough I am thinking about how I
could be a good parent
When I was young I was just like the kids around
Had friends and was free to go to them with no bound.

I had a strict but loving father
My mama until now is a concerned and caring mother
They were both hard workers
I lived a life of simplicity but I was a joker.

I loved to play tricks with my family members
I was always the star dancer
With one foot left on the floor at the center
But what made me go further was their laughter.

I was a favorite niece of my uncles
My Papa Eking, Papa Abang and Tatay Lalo
Papa Andong, Tiyo Duardo and Tiyo Nilo and all
But fore mentioned above had rested in a doom.

My favorite storyteller was my grandma
I had a good time listening to the stories of my lola
Every evening after dinner we had a session at the sala
The legendary folk began to relay the characters of an
old diwata.

It's very nice to reminisce about the happy past
We did not belong in a family of a wealthy clutch
But the footprints of happiness were too much
My younger years were remembered a lot.

These were the times of molding years
I was honed by my family was worth remembering
The time of my younger years I enjoyed much
however
This will last until I become older.

When I was young I experienced a bailehan on the
ground
I went to some barangay fiestas and towns
I went some picnics on the nearby beaches around
But what went on, I was always a conservative gal in
the downtown.

TEACHERS

We are the molders of the future
In our hands lie the souls of the miniature
We can make or unmake them on or before
But the continuity and passion we prolong.

We have encountered so many challenges
A lot of them give us the courage
To pursue our advocacy, the vocation at a merge
Viva! teachers, we are the idols of the children.

We are working beyond our job description
We don't mind our own but look forward to our
inspiration
The lil minds of the children looking up to us with
admiration
Believing in our abilities and capacitation.

Our tenacious intent goes toward the endpoint
The love for our work is the weapon that sent
The meaningful color of the rainbow that bent
From the north to south and east to west.

Teachers, our love never stops
From the start to the last drop
Of blood that runs in the nerves of a hero's treetop
We are the living evidence who don't leave the crop.

Now and forever we are the teachers
Who sow the seeds of knowledge that scatter
To the young minds of these education seekers
We are the pillars who standstill the test of time
forever.

THE VOICE OF FOREVER

I can hear some voices in the midst of a silent night
I can see your voice in your glimmering eyes
I can read the words on your lips that glimpse
I can sing the song of one moment in time.

I offer you the sweet humming lullaby
I take a walk while waiting for the voice to say hi
I can live, I can love, I can fly up to the sky
I realize the truth and the deepest meaning of life.

The voice of forever is somewhere
In the light that shines anywhere
In the air that whispers to our ears
And in the sea breeze beneath the ocean fair.

I am not a poet who can compose a poem so easily
Or either a journalist who writes a featured novel
convincingly
I am a teacher who loves to teach the children
promptly
For the voice of forever is in me.

I love to do the things I wanna do
I want to explore my humble life the way I go
All these things are part of the distinguished You
The creator of the Earth whom we owe.

Follow the voice that commands you
It's God's Holy Gospel in the bible that reminds you
The voice that warns you
And the revelation of truth that saves you.

I was looking for the voice of forever
From my younger years til now, I am older
It is very near yet so far to reach or never
For it brings the good news that hinders our Earthly
matters.

I AM YOURS AND YOU ARE MINE

From the day that I was born
I was destined to be yours alone
And you are mine in return
We are both for each other as a whole.

I love you more than anything can do
Your love for me is the best gift I ever had in life and
so
You are mine as God gave me you
I am yours as a reciprocation of me to you.

Our kids are the evidence of my unending love for
you
Every day is a great renewal of our vows and I do
My prayer goes each day: God grant us a long life for
me and you
For our dear children, they may live a Godly life as
they grow.

Though we are not rich our love outreached
To the nerves of our human systems at best
My kilig factor every time I look at you insists
Yehey! My love believes me at my wildest.

God bless us every now and then
Our faith in him is coupled with our sincere trust in
him
The blessings that will last through the millennial
trends
We are the old folks in the modern refinement.

CHILDREN

They are the gift of God to their parents
They have their own rights and responsibilities
Let us hear and listen to their ideas every now and
then
For they are pure and genuine.

In their offenses, there must be a reason behind
Don't ignore but investigate why it happens
They are the living evidence of our existence
They are the answer to our prayers that give us
challenges.

Children, you are who you are today
But tomorrow we cannot tell who you will become a
day to day
We are a part of building your future into who you
want to be
And it is our great duty and responsibility.

To see you better in the coming days
Is our true and fulfilling feeling of happiness
We are now making a process
To let you be at the peak of success.

HAPPINESS

Is the absolute contentment of something
It's the climax of certainty that something brings
Whether it's little or big as long as it makes you glad
then happiness is occurring
The fulfilment of every detail that life makes you very
achieving.

Happiness with a family is my number one aim
To live, to laugh, and most especially to love with
them
To be with truest friends every day seems
To hold on with each other, the one I love so much is
my enormous happiness for a lifetime.

Happiness with God's blessings is sacred and
rewarding
Happiness that you hurt no one but offering friendship
and love sharing
the one that everybody should celebrate and have a
deep meaning
Happiness that uplifts our hearts beating

The smiles that open every window of housekeeping.
Be happy and contented with what you have
Live with your own means and let the God above
Shower his blessings and turn your half-baked
happiness into success and love

Then you can feel that true happiness is everything we
have.
Be completely happy and feel the essence of God's
presence
Blame no one, accept the fact of your level and have a
glance
To the uppermost happiness that you can have as you
take the chance
Congratulations because happiness governs you
throughout your life not once.

FAMILY

It is a treasure that you keep on
In your blood, it runs all around
Your immediate family is your lifebuoy as the days go
on
You are one whatever goes on

When you're away from your immediate family, your
mother and siblings
As if you are anchored in the midst of the ocean
hanging
Nobody to call on, if you are sick still strive to rise for
surviving
OH! That's how I value my family as I go on living.

Family doesn't count every help you extend to one
another
It is continuous from the day of our birth
Through ups and downs, you are together
How I miss my family, my mother, and my sisters.

Now that we are away from each other
If I don't feel well I just cry and cover
My achy head and muscles are so painful I can't resist
but shiver
Yes my family I love you all how I wish we are near.

The care, the love, and concern you share
It keeps me roaring in my mind and soul so dear
Family is very essential to me Oh! How I wish you
were all here
Living together in the core of forever.

MY PATH

You are my guide when I'm almost lost
You are my inspiration to my post
You are my everlasting boss
You are my light in the midst of dark meadows.

You are my path that I should follow
Throughout my life, you are my shadow
I fear nothing but I feel at ease because of you
My path, my guide my long-time rendezvous.

I wonder why how things get done
In the middle of somewhere, they were gone
But in my mindset, they are far behind
Because of you my path I confessed thy will be done.

To be obedient in all your commandments is my
promise
I am so sorry if I can't make it perfect
But on the lawn of your premise
I follow it more or less.

There you are my path
Who is always ready to catch
When I fall into a wide scratch
My path I'm still on the right path.

RAINFALL

Water droplets from heaven above
If you get wet put yourself a robe
But if you are so vulnerable enough
Equip yourself with a raincoat of love.

Rainfall your sound is so annoying
The rhythm of your fall is so disgusting
But you bring hope to a plant go fading
You are in between the beneficial and harmful use you
bring.

You are a part of a tropical cyclone
The farmers wait for you to come into town
When the beautiful flowers are fading down
You give them hope to live, to abound.

When you are falling so strong flooding occurs
You can destroy properties of ours
You must be moderate in all aspects of yours
Be there sooner or later but don't abuse.

Rainfall is the best example of a cycle
The unending rotation of water in the middle
Of the process, it comes little by little
But sometimes it pours so full overflowed at all.

THE BUSY BEE

On the grassy mini-park
Here goes the busy bee at large
What's the essence of being in the dark?
When one likes you always sparks.

Busy bee when will you be mine
Your time and attention reminds
I really long to be with you in due time
But you have all in the midst of line.

Your voice is so slow and nothing shows
The concern and thoughts don't blow
For your emotions so strong enough to draw
Why can't you make it so true.

I wonder why you do it alike
When I have shown you in spike
Different feelings that everyone tried
That is you a busy bee invites.

The more busy bees in the street
The lesser they take a bit
Maybe because you mind the lit
You are not so sensitive to uplift.

JOCKEY, MY PET DOG

Seventeen years of existence
Living with our family thru thick and thin
Our pet dog who was ever loyal to us on all points
He was our pet who thought like a human being.

Jockey is a black dog with white pigments
He was a very good friend.
He never forgot to bless and say amen
During Angelus after the bell ringing.

Not only once twice nor thrice that he traveled alone
Crossing the Hinatuan River on his own
He ran, jumped, and rest finding our location
Jockey traveled a long-long way on.

There was a time when my father played a song
Jockey cried aloud towards the cassette playing on
OH! Jockey why do you feel that come on
He was like us, had feelings and had emotions.

He was also an expert in opening the doorknob
He shouted loud when somebody wants to rob
He was our trusted house guard
Jockey your a lone kind of dog we had.

My Jockey at seventeen became weak
This must be the long life span of a dog's existence
When I went home one summer my Jockey was no
longer alert
He had a skinny backbone with no hair.

The following year I heard from my father and mother
My Jockey was gone he was no longer here
He didn't eat and sleep forever
This was the story of our pet dog Jockey dear.

CITY LIFE

Every day we're in a hurry
Keep coping the time for work every day
If you can't, you might get late daily
Traffic awaits you all the way.

The fruits and fish we buy
In the market they display
We are not sure if they are really
Fresh and suitable for our needs and commodities.

Some people here depend on
Ready-made and cooked food
For they are tired and have no time to cook
City life is fast and tiresome.

Go on living in the city
This is what God wants us to be
As long as we are happy with our family
Let's be there as long as time tell me
We are the living legends of life in the city.

Here children are taught properly
But some of them go differently
They are influenced by modern technology
That gives them super energy.

Life in the city is different from the province
A complicated and more sophisticated
But anyone and everyone dreams
To dwell in the city they think of heaven.

HONESTY

Why don't you tell me the truth?
The word honesty as I seek about
This is the simplest way of respect I thought
Bring it to the fullest mind of growth

In every situation, honesty is the process of trust
When you can not how do I give you a lot
In a very small thing, you can not
There's something you hide what's that?

The more you can't bigger than that
I'm almost tired of having a sleepless night
Thinking of anything between us
Please tell me I ought to know about that.

My concern for you goes beyond
Can I have from you even the least one?
This is a feeling of being treated beside
I can't help but cry deep inside.

To all who can read this nothing happens
This is only the fruit of how I imagine
In every scenario of honesty up in
Because honesty symbolizes a faith begins.

SUMMER

Everyone finds fun during summer
They feel loved and ponder
On a very sweet summer temper
The wind blows and sunlight covers.

It's the summer breeze that makes me feel
The love and caress of wind so thrill
Come and celebrate the feast of the summer bell
The waves of the sea that breaks on the seashore's hill.

OH! It's fascinating and reminding of us in there
A group of families wants to swim on a beach of
crystal water
Wow! The bonding marks their lifetime souvenir
You and I have pure fun in summer.

The sun that smiles so wide
It brings attraction to all of us who hide
Come, go out from your shell, and glide
Into the external world of summer rides.

Adventure here and there or everywhere
So much exposure to the beautiful Earth
That's the essence of loving the season of summer
Let's be in love and feel the love we long to go over.

OH!, Summer, you are just once a year
But the joy you bring is worth to remember
We love to explore together forever
Thank God for the summer you bring in here.

EMPTINESS

God will fill the empty feeling
I strive to make myself at ease doing something
I really feel empty cause for you I am longing
This is new to us since then.

To be in distance with my love my only man
Is a terrible feeling of emptiness I've gone
I should do something to keep us one
A united family living together at once.

For what, that we are here?
And you are there...
Because you love to be a farmer
Yes your objectives are all for the better

But what can I do?
I really, really miss you
I support all your plans and view
To fight the emptiness I can not do

God, please help me to be used to
The longer the time the more I miss you
Daddy my love it's true
If I have wings I will fly through

Every day I will do it just to be with you
I am sure you feel the same I know
I have full trust in you
But trusting is not the issue.

It's the emptiness that attacks me
OH!, God, this is not a game only
This is what we call reality
I want to drag the days so easily.

That ocean and forest of trees
That bound us from miles away
Will be transformed to the nearest city
Where we can be together every day.

God bless you, my love daddy
He may protect you from harm daily
And guide you in the best way
To the success of our project someday.

Emptiness is the state of longing
When one is searching for a certain belonging
A time of looking up anything
That you feel not in you at present.

But God has the ultimate answer
Sacrifices will be paid off later
With success and happiness forever
A family that prays constantly will be rewarded.

RIGHTEOUSNESS

We are prone to do mistakes
But the way we are is what we make
Be responsible for all you take
Making it wrong is your risk.

God commands us to love one another
Helping, loving, and nurturing each other
Be sensitive enough to the feelings of your sister
You might put her in a hot water.

Sometimes we do things in a haphazard way
Giving her some blames, she doesn't do anyway
Forgetting all the things she did us positively.
Friendship is wasted in a quick moment

In a futile style, it was gone
Gone naturally, feelings were hurt
Emotions flooded with tears and broken.
Remember my friend we should be righteous

Don't judge her the way you choose
Balance and observance take it and use
You may go in the wrong direction that flows.
Be awakened now, look back from where you started

Pick up the pieces of some fragments
Select and collect but take the useful experience
Junk the ones that drag you in bad influence.
Stand strong, you victim

Find a way to have remorse for your offender
Be righteous God loves us together
Let's join Him hand in hand with one another.

CURIOSITY

It all begins with a question
That sometimes need not listen to an opinion
Most are due to knowing others' concerning behavior
This is mostly misunderstood.

When curiosity strikes it can make us disturbed
Inquiring and asking anything in this world
But the way you ask questions is erroneous
In a way of unethical mood.

Which question is correct?
Ask for curiosity purpose
Or ask a question to be informed
And sometimes in an ambiguous form.

Curiosity strikes the heart of some individuals
They answer questions that are irrelevant
In the sense that they lead to be embarrassed
What is your real and pure purpose?

In my own honest suggestion
In this fragile world, we are not sure
Of anything, anybody anymore
It's God only can assure.

If you are curious about the things around
Try to investigate on your own
Be sure you can't offend on
The way you imply you're question.

CLOUDY DAY

It's not a perfect moment
To witness all these scenes
The high tide climbs on a vine
In the meantime of thy line.

Cheer up sunlight let me see your smile
Take away the cloudy day a while
Ahead of us in this northern side
Bring us back the sweet love of thine.

Cloudy day you're so mysterious
Am not sure the witty picky of yours
Will it rain or shine above us all
May I peep the face of my sweet queen abode.

Luxurious living or any of those high profiles
I need none of them but your cute and pure smile
Unveiling the message of our God's divine
Who possesses everything across thy hidden life.

Poetic line it's not mine
It's just the simplest skyline
Oh from the east and west wind
Blow us in unity and one mind.

The clouds that cover the sunlight
Will soon fall as rain in the midst of time
Go away cloudy day free us from shame
Sunlight gives us authentic brightness.

How I wish I could hold you tight
And take you beside of me all the time
It could be soon or nothing
But God the Father will provide.

LOVE MONTH

Show your love don't hesitate
Love month is here right
It's time for us to celebrate
Don't miss even a single moment.

Bring the joy to the heart
Mind and soul of anyone on Earth
Cherish the love and bring out the best
For you and I have a mind-set.

Love month draws nearer
For lovers are forever
In our lives, we must cheer
The truest love we feel.

Oh love here we are taking our part
In the midst of hindrances inside out
Take hold of the sweetest feelings we impart
The purest love from God.

Home of love, the love month
Loving the man we want
In our life, we offer the one
The most precious like a diamond.

Love month share us now and always
The time, the most joyous memories
Thank God you are the reservoir
Of the love, we have in our inner being.

DELECTATION

On your way to the golden age
Here you go to completeness
The words uttered mean happiness
One day or another it begins with faithfulness.

Hurray! life is full of challenges
Rise now and face these things
Delectation of what you had been
Look up and see the betterment.

Can you not be happy?
Won't you be anyway?
Smile to the back and let it be
Oh, thank God for this life of me.

Count the blessings discard the uncertainty
All of these are God's purity
Never blame him but bear it gratefully
What you are, who you are is you really.

A facade of you is just a cover page
The inner of you is the truest
You can't deny, as if or pretend
The truth will always prevail.

So delectation depends on how you accept
In normal or mediocre ways
Still, oneself is the bearer of contentment
I am searching for the just and finest.

Friendship or any relationship would be erased
If selfishness comes into every heart
The desires of Earthly matters govern
To crawl up to reach the pedestal.

Only God can give us complete delectation
For him, fairness is all the time for a reason
Not like us who do things for ourselves alone.
Remember we are here with some limitations.

CHEER UP

Life is so beautiful
Don't give up on failure
Cheer up for the future
Time is not yet yours.

God is the center of all endeavors
Fight all the lying sides of course
Make it better the way you do all
Positivism is always the best cure.

Sign up and think the bright star
In the sky, it shines like your support bar
Wave high into the highest space and herald
Yours is now and mine is at the top remark.

These are all the tests of time
The examination of perseverance
The trial of high and down
A challenge for one man's trusting heart.

Cheer up God is with you all the time
Never think of failures done
Be joyful about all the things we had
Be merry and spread the love.

CHRISTMAS SEASON

When I was young I looked at you differently
I thought you were just a display
Of new dresses, parols, and even emotionally
Now that I'm getting older I see the meaning clearly.

The Christmas season is more about giving and
forgiving
It's not just a material but more on spiritual messaging
All we do are an only facade of what we are
celebrating
Get the ultimate and the real meaning.

Christmas is a season of love and sharing
Let's do our part of loving and caring
To the child lying in the crib of Bethlehem
Jesus is the reason for all of these happenings.

But to be merry and happy we should
For it is the essence of Christmas hood
A term I invented now as I could
The union of everybody as God told.

SACRIFICIAL MOMENTS

When and how you sacrifice
It's about time to let us find
The sacrifices we made regard us high
Though we don't mean to tell a lie

Sacrificial moments doing things beyond your
comfort zone
A matter that makes you forget in the meanwhile of
your own
A time to make a change that you simply do on
Day by day or habitual as the days go on.

Why should we do it?
Because God himself did the sacrificial moment
When Jesus Christ offered
His life on the cross he laid.

Living in this world is full of challenges
Every single day connotes a change
That change may be favorable or nays
That's a point of a sacrificial moment.

All of us have this point in time
To undergo a sacrificial moment for yours and mine
Don't give up God provides the perfect line
To follow thru as we go all while.

Be patient in doing your sacrificial moments
For you can't tell the time it ends
Maybe an hour, a day, a month, or years
What's essential is you are aware.

This is in different forms
But surely you are not informed
The time it comes in your life upon
Be prepared God gives us a complete duration.

ABOUT THE AUTHOR

DR. JEARDINE Q. SANTOS is recently a Master Teacher in Manuel Luis Quezon Elementary School teaching Science for almost 20 years. She holds her professional license as a teacher since 2001.

She got Married to Gemwell R. Santos, with 4 kids namely; Jenea Ghem. Tristan Lhee, Ken Amhir and Jhulio Jemkhenlee.

She is the proud daughter of Adelaida O. Quenano and the late Federico P. Quenano.

Jeardine's hobby includes making Poems.

Jeardine took her college education of her course Bachelor in Elementary Education(BEED) in Pangasinan State University Bayambang Campus and graduated in the year 2001.

Her Graduate Studies include; Master of Arts in Education Major in Educational Management with Thesis(MAED) at New Era University in 2007, and doctor of Education Major in Educational Management with Dissertation (EDD) in New Era University in 2010.

Her accomplishments and recognitions are; Division Module Writer in ESP II, Division Facilitator, District Trainer/Winner in 2019, Most Outstanding MLQES Master Teacher in 2020, School Pag-asa sa Basura Coordinator in 2019 to the Present, School Boy Scout Member and National Bronze Awardee in 2016 to the Present, E-SIP Member and Project Facilitator in 2021 to the Present, School LDM2 LAC Leader, School LAC Leader, School Yes-O Adviser for 2 years, School INSET Chairperson-2022, School INSET Speaker and Master Teacher In Charge of YES-O, ESP for Grade 5 and Grade 6 Teachers,

www.ingramcontent.com/pod-product-compliance
Lightning Source LLC
LaVergne TN
LVHW020932200726
843506LV00011B/1945